How to Stop Overthinking

7 Steps to Silence Your Inner Critic, Build Unshakable Self-Confidence, and Calm Your Overactive Mind

Howard Hudson

Table of Contents

Introduction

The mind is its own place, and in itself, can make a heaven out of Hell, a hell out of Heaven. –John Milton

Overthinking is a double-edged sword. On the one hand, it can help us work smarter, not harder by urging us to engage in effective problem-solving in short amounts of time. On the other hand, overthinking can make us doubt, question and over-analyze every single thing that has ever happened to us in our lives. For example, overthinking leads to creating intrusive and fake scenarios in our heads in reaction to something that was said to us that day. I might have received a comment along the lines of "That top looks crazy," when wearing a colorful shirt with loud patterns. To the other person, it was a harmless comment made in the heat of the moment. But to me, the overthinker, it was an open-captioned statement that will be analyzed until I can find the meaning and intentions behind it. I will undoubtedly lay awake all night, my mind running in infinite circles to unravel the "complex" comment, until I have found a conclusion to its intention and have finally found satisfaction in deciphering the innocent comment. Only then, am I able to sleep peacefully.

In another example, I may have an upcoming event that I feel unprepared for, like a gala or work seminar. In the weeks following up to the event, I may find myself thinking about it a lot; analyzing what might happen, how I might respond to certain questions (should I meet someone), *will I even meet someone new? Will people even like me? How will I spend my off days leading up to the event? Where should I get lunch or dinner?* I could also find myself scouring the boutiques near my home for something to wear in advance, "practice" social cues (such as when to make a joke or how to carry myself in terms of posture), research the topics that may be brought up, or try to make friends with the co-workers accompanying me so that I at least have a friend. These are just some of the examples that run through an overthinker's head when certain situations arise.

But, however awful it may sound, it's not all bad; overthinking can heighten productivity and act as an inner motivator, inspiring a drive to achieve goals I would have never thought were possible of achieving. Overthinking can help us make decisions, see things from another perspective, and gain clarity on subjects that might have been difficult to understand at that moment. That's the beauty of overthinking. When it's good, it's beautiful, inspiring, and motivational. But when it's bad, it's dehumanizing, disappointing, and discouraging. It's a double-edged sword and it has no wielder, it's an entity entirely on its own.

The Science Behind Overthinking

Overthinking not only affects our motivation and the way we perceive things, but it also has a scientific effect on our brains. To better understand what happens to our brains during the inescapable trap of overthinking, we need to take a look at a few key characters. The first character is dopamine. The "feel good" hormone is mainly in charge of regulating the way we feel pleasure. When our brains have a healthy amount of dopamine we feel positive emotions, and we learn quicker. High levels of dopamine also increase our need to be social and can turn the deepest introvert into an exploding extrovert for the benefit of our mental health. Creativity is also simulated by the neurotransmitter and influences the amount of empathy we feel for others.

It's all fun and games until dopamine deficiency hits and all of that goes out the window. Because the effects of high levels of dopamine can be compared to some form of earthly heaven, the deficiency must be like hell; it can cause loss of interest in things we once enjoyed, influence behavior for the worse, rob us of our sleep, decrease motivation, decrease productivity, and cause anxiety.

The next culprit, and one I didn't suspect at first, is cortisol. While dopamine is the gray between good and evil, cortisol is the ultimate villain in this story. As the primary stress hormone, high levels of cortisol can cause heart problems, headaches, concentration problems, and a list of other health issues. Cortisol is released by the hypothalamus that senses the levels of cortisol in the blood and directs the brain to act accordingly. In reaction to a deficiency, the brain then adjusts the number of hormones it makes, and the adrenal glands increase the amount of cortisol they make—in turn, making us more stressed than usual.

Our bodies are literally turning against our minds unintentionally. Because of increased levels of cortisol due to hormone levels being "out of whack," our minds are "exposed" to the sick cycle of unhealthy overthinking to worm its way into our life.

Stress is the biggest contributor to analysis-paralysis and not as easily controlled as society wants us to believe. It cannot be controlled by a bubble bath or a scented candle; life has never been that glamorous. And it is no secret that modern day adults are confronted with serious issues out of our control. Everyone has to deal with global warming that is leaving our planet in ruins, the pandemic that (literally) ended our social lives for years, the world economy that is slowly declining, living costs that keep rising above the average earnings of our households, and many other things that cause subconscious stress and weariness on both our minds and bodies.

However, while our minds can be our worst enemies, they can also be our greatest weapons. Located at the back of the eyes and in front of the hypothalamus, lies the orbitofrontal cortex (aka, the secret weapon) that can be modified with daily activities to the point where it can lessen overall stress levels and heighten optimism. By making use of learning activities, mind puzzles, and anything that exercises the brain, we can impact the amount of stress our bodies generate in the form of cortisol. These activities thicken the orbitofrontal cortex, which in turn (almost like a thank you) blocks a large amount of the cortisol receptors from receiving their signals—no "stress" is being generated. It has been proven that people with a thinner orbitofrontal cortex experience higher salivary cortisol level as opposed to people with a thicker cortex; they are also generally more optimistic and highly motivated.

In conclusion, we are technically not in charge or responsible for the mental cage we find ourselves in 24/7; the mind unintentionally places us in this position by doing its job. However, I have the power to change the outcome of this situation by making use of strategies and tips to take back my power and reclaim my own mind, making it work in favor of me and my goals, and not against me.

I have lost count of the many times I have heard "Stop thinking about it," in my lifetime. But I think science has done the talking for me today. Overthinking isn't merely "thinking." It is the uncontrollable over-analyzation of events that drains every ounce of joy from people.

Chapter 1:

Changing the Narrative in

Your Head

The mind has a powerful way of attracting things in harmony with it, good and bad. —Idowu Koyenikan

At the beginning of every rom-com, there is a voice explaining everything that leads up to that moment. It tells us details about the character's life and feelings; sometimes they'll even explain what happens after the timeline of the movie. In our lives, that narrator is "me." The only difference is that the movie was pre-written, and we are actively writing our destiny as we go about our lives.

I can alter the way my life is going to play out by the way I carry myself, how I react to things, the relationships I build and how long they will last, the decisions I make and where they will take me. I can change the whole course of my life with something as seemingly unimportant as the way I dress and talk. But most importantly, and the thing that makes the biggest impact, is the state of my mindset.

Let's face it, the world around us is full of people who are strategically placed at certain points of our lives to either change it for the better, make an impact on us, or ruin it; the good thing is that we can decide. For example, Mr. Bigman CEO strolls into the office that I have worked at for five years, and he fires me based on one poorly written report or on a far-fetched idea he was disappointed he didn't think of earlier. This is a life-altering moment, and I have two choices. I can pack up the very few things in my office and either find another job for the same amount of money while lowering my head in shame or silence the voice inside my head screaming, *You're a loser!* and replace the aggressive, discouraging monologue of my mind into a peaceful and understanding dialogue between me and myself about the next steps that await.

How to Silence Your Inner Voice and Flip the Script on Your Thinking

I have always wondered how the voice inside my mind is its own entity. It knows all of the things I am about to do before I do them, and it knows every lyric to every song I've ever heard or heard for the first time, and it can never be quiet. How does that small voice inside my head obsessively practice every detail of a story before I tell it? Why does it create and then solve problems all on its own? Why does it go out of its incorporeal way to sing "Barbie Girl" on a continuous loop at 3 am in the morning? Well, the answer is simple, but complex.

The mind believes in itself and itself alone. Your mind is programmed to believe that we are completely made up of "mind" and that there is nothing else to it. Therefore, when it does one day decide to shut up, there would be nothing but dead space. It'll be oblivion if you will. If the mind cannot experience and explore itself through the act of thinking and narrating, it simply does not exist. By creating the image of "me" in consciousness, it can maintain the experience of itself and the experiencer (physical me) in which both are necessary to survival, otherwise there would be death, or vegetative state.

By making use of this constant narrative, the mind actively realizes that the events in our lives as true, tangible experiences, rather than an unpredictable figment of the imagination. We are thinking ourselves into existence in the world around us. Our minds are making us "real" to the world, present, representative. This is exactly why a healthy mindset is so important for building a healthy relationship with overthinking and our inner selves. If the mind is strong enough to "think" us into existence, imagine what it can do for our overall health if we can use it properly in a way that benefits us.

Strategies to Change the Narrative in Your Head

How do I change the narrative to benefit me? With the simple act of thinking. I get it; it's like trying to change the color of a pot by rubbing another one against it. But it's true; the simple act of redirecting the thoughts that plague us into either positive or neutral waters is the first thing that's going to set our minds on track for the change that is coming. However, the difficult part is catching our minds in the heat of negativity and nipping it in the bud before it goes from a cuddly kitty to a roaring lion.

Make Use of Your Senses

One strategy that has been proven to actively redirect the mind is the conscious action of taking in every sensory change I can. When I notice my mind is at its worst, I pause, take a breath, and absorb all of the five senses available to me. *Hear* five things, *smell* five things, *touch* five things, *taste* five things, *see* five things, and sense my physical state as I am in that moment.

This works for two reasons. For one, this will take my mind off of the subject I am dwelling on and redirect it into a more neutral area where I will be open to a more positive route or mental change. Second, it isn't completely distracting me from the problem and creating unhealthy avoidance habits, it is simply allowing my mind to reassess the severity of the problem. I assess how I may solve it without leaving me restless at two o'clock in the morning. This is about finding the calm in the eye of the storm around me.

Be Self-Aware

Being self-aware is one way to make the change subconsciously. I control how I receive and process information, and how I feed it into my mind. Picture this: I'm on my way home from work after a long day and the boss unexpectedly calls me, demanding I come back to the office to work on another poorly explained project. This is the crossroad where I can now decide to make the change. Either I put on a brave face and control the negative thoughts already swirling in the thunder clouds around my brain, blowing them away with the wind of positivity and affirmation (for example, I love my job), or I can fall back into the familiar comfort of negativity. If I chose the former, I have successfully taken a situation that would have caused mental flat spin and overthinking and paved the way for mental healing.

The work cannot only be done by my mind automatically. I am going to have to put in conscious work of stopping my negative thinking in the moment and redirect it to another route in order to overcome or prevent overthinking. If I had not made the decision to think positively and returned to the office in a poor mood, I would have wasted at least four hours of my time thinking about the situation. I could have avoided it by just not answering my phone; I could have spent this time by watching episodes of my favorite show. Ultimately it would have worsened my already bad mood. Overthinking is not just about analyzing bad experiences or anticipating what's to come, it is the overthinking of every situation in our lives that can possibly affect the quality of our lives as a whole.

Focus On Problem-Solving Rather Than Problem-Obsessing

While overthinking, it's easy to believe that I have no other way out and that any decision I make will be the wrong one. I am under the impression that my mind is working out a way to solve the problems I have in my life when it's actually just overanalyzing every aspect of it with no problem-solving in sight. My mind is in panic mode, and I have no idea what to do about the problem before me. That's the cunning nature of overthinking, it sneaks in under the illusion of problem-solving and sinks its nasty claws into unsuspecting me. But the bright side is that I can stop overthinking from happening in the first place. By focusing all of my energy on finding solutions, my mind is redirecting itself from the state of panic, back into a position where it can be useful. However, if I can't consciously pull myself back from the chaos, I can make use of the following questions to get my mind back on track.

1. What is the root problem?

2. How can I solve it?

3. When do I take action to solve it?

Answering these simple questions will help me gain clarity on the subject, discern the "important" from the "irrelevant" and pinpoint the severity of the problem. From there, I will be able to remain calm until my problem dissipates. You see, by human nature, we crave discipline and routine. Therefore, every time we experience a minor setback out of our usual routine, we experience panic and a sense of chaos, especially when it comes to things we can't see coming. For example, the internet may go out when we crunch for a deadline. In some instances, like the weather, we can prepare our minds for the possibility of many different scenarios, and it can prepare solutions for when the problem does arise at a leisurely pace. But when our minds do not have the courtesy of preparing for a possible setback, it can go into panic mode with the snap of a finger. Unexpected setbacks combined with unhealthy mental habits makes the perfect blend for an overthinking cocktail. But in this scene, I am the bartender and I get to decide what's being served.

Talk to Someone

With all the talking our minds are doing, it seems fair that we should be allowed to talk too. One of the best ways to reflect on our struggles is with a friend or a diary (the latter doesn't judge, so do what you will with that). Airing out all of the anxiety and stress we feel over a steaming cup of coffee or a beer with a friend might just be what we've been missing. It's easy to convince ourselves that what we are feeling is minor in comparison to the worldly struggles of other people. Because of that, we might get discouraged and fall deeper into the trap of overthinking. But the simple act of acknowledging our struggles might prompt our friends to relate, and both parties might find release from knowing neither of us are alone.

There is power in the act of seeking advice from friends or loved ones; there is beauty in the acceptance of our struggles and knowing that despite what our minds might tell us, we will overcome this sick cycle. Humans are social creatures by nature, we crave the pleasure of acceptance and camaraderie, and it might be just the thing we need to gain perspective. Listening to our problems from another perspective, and how our friends might solve our problems can open up the door to clarity regarding a certain situation. Wisdom can come in many shapes and forms, even frat buddy Jason or bubbly Britney.

Chapter Takeaways

It is extremely difficult to rewire our minds to think in a way that has been foreign to them up until this moment, especially considering they all share the notion that they are "superior." It will take time, and it will not happen overnight; but by making use of the strategies that have been discussed in this chapter, we can all start the journey to a better mental lifestyle and overcome our overthinking.

- Make the change mentally to alter the course of my life for the better.

- Make use of my senses to ground myself in order to avoid or overcome overthinking; hear, see, smell, taste, and touch five things, and anchor myself in that present moment.

- Make changes according to the reactions I allow myself to have, whether they are positive or negative.

- Change my mindset from problem-obsessing to problem-solving by answering the three core questions:

  1. What is the root problem?

  2. How do I solve it?

  3. When do I take action to solve it?

- Confide in someone about my problem with overthinking and receive advice to open myself up to new perspectives.

Chapter 2:

Look Toward What's Coming and Not What Has Passed

You never know ahead of time what something is really going to be like. —Katherine Paterson

Picture this: I'm in bed with freshly washed linens, both sides of my pillow are cold. I'm just about to drift off to sleep when my mind decides to play the perfect compilation of my life's most embarrassing moments, dating back to my childhood days, just for the extra cringe. Believe it or not, but this is a form of overthinking that causes even more overthinking. We all know that I will then flip through the pages of my life's book and highlight sections and situations where I would have communicated a bit clearer, given it a bit more finesse, had more fun, or avoided a situation altogether. As it is with everything else in the world, we never truly realize the significance of a moment until it has passed. That's the beauty of the past: It inevitably comes to pass, and we all only have one shot to make it truly memorable, one way or another.

The Fake Security of the Past

The past sells a fake sense of security to each of us, a small bubble of familiarity to fall back on when the uncertainty of the future gets too scary. It's difficult to let go of the past; it's an incorporeal album of experiences, memories, and people that we have collected over the span of our lives. We will continue to collect until we inevitably cease to exist. It is also the most familiar thing we have. The past is full of lessons and situations we have already experienced and know the outcome of. Therefore, there is no window for further stress as it has already happened. Think about it; because we have already run the course of a certain situation, we don't have the usual anxiety linked to our thought process like we do with unknown scenarios and changes that may come my way. Because we have already experienced all of the events of our past, our mind recognizes the familiarity of it and is instantly comforted.

But, however comforting that thought may be, we still run the risk of overthinking. When I'm overthinking, I will not only remember every good and bad event that has happened to me, but I will also be reminded of every single regret I have had in my life. The embarrassing moment when I accidentally overshared with my crush or a random stranger, or when I stumbled late into a meeting; even the regret of letting the opportunity of a lifetime pass me by out of fear of the unknown will come racing back. And with it, every emotion, and every strategy on how I can avoid the situation in the future. And while it's a part of our "programming" to become wiser from our mistakes and lessons in life, reflecting too much on one thing is a sure-fire way of getting caught in the cycle of overthinking.

The Freedom of Forgiveness

Some argue that the best way to cure myself of the hurts of the past is to forgive and forget, but it's not quite that easy. Forgiveness is a gift that is rarely given. It's given only when the giver is so completely healed and mentally advanced that they realize forgiveness for the benefit of their own spiritual health. However, the freedom that comes with utter forgiveness is something few people get to experience in their lifetime. It is pure and utter disappearance of hurt and any unresolved feelings one might have had regarding a certain situation. I am free of the overthinking that has plagued my thoughts from one simple act of forgiveness. Sure, the forgiveness was given out of selfish reasons, but aren't humans self-centered by nature? We do most of the things in our life to secure the survival of *our* species don't we? If we cannot forgive the person who has wronged us for the benefit of relieving their guilt, we can give it to the person or situation for the benefits of ourselves.

With the forgiveness comes the relief of the overthinking that was further worsened by the lingering displeasure of the situation. If we have completely eliminated the lingering emotions of the event, we have eliminated the worries that came with it—along with the overthinking piggybacking on it.

The Importance of Balance

Unresolved feelings or confusion around a certain subject is one of the core causes of overthinking. Humans are inquisitive beings by nature. We're designed with the desire to learn and understand things in order to further evolve our species. Therefore, when something happens unexpectedly, we tend to obsess over it until it is either resolved or beyond our knowledge. Because of that, it is important to remember that not all overthinking is unhealthy. The imbalance of it all is what makes it unhealthy. It's exactly the same with everything else. A glass of wine is just fine, but a few bottles of wine a night is unhealthy. A few beers with my friends every Friday night is just fine, but a few beers with my friends every day is unhealthy. In moderation, overthinking is a great way to focus on problem-solving, can help us make fast decisions based on facts, and in some cases, it can actually help the "thinker" solve a difficult problem they have been struggling with. It all depends on finding the right balance.

To find the right balance in our overthinking schedules, we have to assess what the correct amount of "thinking" is. If we spend hours on one problem and cannot find any viable outcome, it might be better to leave it alone for some time to rest, reflect, and try again. But if we continuously analyze the current state of the problem, with no rest, change, or solution, we might be stuck in the cycle of overthinking once again. Basically, if it robs me of my peace of mind, I know it's overthinking and not problem-solving. Find the balance.

Stop Obsessing Over Your Mistakes

Finding a balance between learning from our mistakes and dwelling on them, however, is a whole other scenario. Mistakes have always been viewed as lessons learned. They are great opportunities to grow and shape a newer, improved me, but they can also be so severe that I find myself unable to forgive myself for making them. When we experience guilt regarding a mistake or decision, it's difficult to just let it go and move on. We often find ourselves searching for other ways to reconcile with the mistake. Obviously, that's not going to happen. The best we can do is to just acknowledge that we are human (mistakes will always be made) and ensure that they don't happen again in the future. But in the severe cases where the overthinking cloud has come to rain on my parade, I try to make use of the following strategies.

Get Some Space

In the situation where we make a mistake, nine out of ten times there are always witnesses. It's the universe's way of giving us the finger (sadly) because there is nothing more horrifying than having someone witness us in our lowest moment. I might want to curse and burst out in tears; but because of someone staring at me from across the hallway, I can't react in the way I truly want to; therefore, this moment haunts me until the end of my days.

When I mean "get some space," I don't mean running away from our problems; that's never a good way to solve any problem. The best way to truly learn from our mistakes is to first detach ourselves from the situation emotionally and reflect on it from our "other" perspectives. We have to forget about the first-hand embarrassment and what people might think of us, forget about the consequences of our mistakes, and whether or not it's the end of the world (because we'll always feel like it is). Instead, it is better to find clarity in another perspective and we might find that the problem isn't nearly as big as we thought; and if it is, we are now in the perfect position to make a level-headed, neutral decision on how to fix it. This is where the healthy part of overthinking comes to play.

I truly believe that I am sometimes unable to reach my full potential because of the fear that has been instilled in me due to mistakes that have not properly been addressed. It doesn't always have to be a public "fix" to get our co-workers' approval or erasure of lingering "highlights" of our mistakes; it can be an inner acceptance and forgiveness toward ourselves, from ourselves. That's where we learn from the mistake instead of just obsessing over it and creating irrational fear that will continue to fester like an infected wound.

Distraction

Unlike on the basis of overthinking, distraction is a good thing. If I can't bring myself to try active problem-solving soon after a "situation," it's best to distract myself from it completely to give myself and my mind a break. However, going on the phone for five hours straight isn't what I would recommend, as it just leaves the window open for another (although slightly calmer) "draft" of overthinking to drift in.

Giving my mind something to concentrate on will challenge my brain and "reset" its thinking default. Filling out a simple crossword puzzle, jogging, reading an article on the newest fashion trends, and making designer clothes from cheaper materials will succeed in rerouting my mind into "problem-solving" mode as opposed to "panic" mode. Activities like paced jogging or yoga breathing exercises have been known to calm minds that are prone to overthinking because of their "present-moment"-focused natures that demand the wandering mind to return to focus in order to complete the activity.

We must take care, nurture, and give breaks to our minds. Distracting ourselves from our mistakes will give our minds the chance they need to think rationally, to decide if the mistake is as bad as we think, and to make peace with it.

Whine About It

The oldest form of "venting" is whining. There is absolutely nothing wrong with whining for five minutes, especially when I'm embarrassed.

I am the biggest whiner anyone will ever meet. It doesn't matter as long as I get it out. The truest form of torture, to me personally, is keeping something that is bothering me, all to myself; and I stand by that. If I can find the courage to air my mistakes and embarrassment to a loved one, they can usually relate to every emotion

I am feeling, and it empowers me. Another simple science fact that can explain why I am empowered by their relation to my problem is the following: In the psychological part of our programming, as soon as our loved ones relate to our problems, we automatically feel better

1. because they survived this exact moment, as they are sitting right across from me, so there is hope at the end of this dark tunnel.

2. because they have dealt with it before and can give me advice on how to handle it without worrying myself to death.

3. because it just feels better to know that I am not alone and that these things happen to all of us.

4. because you don't feel as dramatic about it as before. Typically, we constantly compare our problems to the bigger problems of the world and don't allow ourselves to acknowledge our own struggles.

I like to remind myself of these few facts every time I feel bad about whining. *No, you are not selfish or a cry baby; you are human. It's completely normal to want to "whine" about a bad day, a horrible mistake, or an embarrassing moment, or even just in general. There is nothing wrong with it, and don't let anybody tell you differently; just keep it within bounds.* It has worked wonders.

Chapter Takeaways

The past is difficult to leave alone, but with the correct measures in place to secure our own mental health regarding the past, we won't have to avoid it anymore. Remember to

- leave the past behind.

- forgive myself if I cannot yet forgive others.

- create a balance between healthy and unhealthy overthinking and when to distinguish between the two.

- not obsess over my mistakes, or else I'll make my anxiety worse.

- detach myself from the situation emotionally and gain a new perspective.

- distract myself for the time being until I can think clearly.

- whine about it; get it out to forget about it and move on.

Chapter 3:

Focus on What You Can

Control

Life is to be lived, not controlled; and humanity is won by continuing to play in face of certain defeat. –Ralph Ellison

I have found myself feeling so hopelessly out of hand that I obsess over every little thing in my life that I can control. I find myself clutching onto the illusion of control so much that I lose my mind every time anything unexpected happens. This is a common trait of every overthinker on this planet and is the perfect habitat for the overthinking monster dwelling in the swamps of our brain.

We cannot control every single thing in our lives; it's a fact. It may be a sad fact, because most of us have planned our lives since we were twelve. There are too many unpredictable factors in life for our plans to turn out exactly how we pictured them to. For example, when we were little, we pictured ourselves growing up to be a fireman, policeman, princess, veterinarian, doctor, (and for the politically ambitious) the president of a country. But then life happened, and some of us didn't get the test scores we needed, we found out the closest thing to a princess in the real world are the cosplay stars at VidCon, or some of us just lost the passion we once had. If some of us are old enough to remember living through 2019—2022, we were caught in a worldwide pandemic that derailed billions of people's careers, education, ambitions, and in some cases, even our will to live.

There is no surefire way to solidify every single aspect of our life into a secure outcome. Therefore, we have to focus on what we can control so we allow ourselves grace in the situations that we can't control.

How to Focus on What I Can Control

Mindfulness

Acknowledging that I cannot be in control of everything is the first step to empowering myself for change. Mindfulness is the simple act of realizing my power in this world and making peace with the aspects of my life where I am powerless. It is the act of being present with where I am in that moment (both physically and mentally) to make way for observations done within myself to alter my behavior. In response, our reactions and emotions toward specific situations can be altered to better impact our minds and lessen the feelings of powerlessness.

Awareness of Our Thoughts and Feelings

Believe it or not, but we are not completely in control of our thoughts or our feelings, we are only in control of our responses to these feelings. Each of these mental and spiritual experiences have "minds" of their own because they are not wired to be polite and say what people want to hear; they are purely wired to respond and relay what our truest beings are tuned to say. Therefore, we find ourselves blushing at the "rude" thoughts in our head and correct them after realizing where our minds have strayed.

Being aware of our thoughts and feelings is the closest thing to "control" we'll ever have over these "entities." What we can control, however, are our reactions and corrections toward them. For example, turning negative thoughts neutral or positive. If we are actively rewiring our minds from one mindset to the other, there will be significant changes not only to our physical and mental health, but also to the environment around us. Positive "vibes" attract opportunities and maybe even a few new friends; negative "vibes" attract demotivational situations and people and ultimately just "sucky" things in general.

If I can "get a grip" on my emotions before they spiral out of my control, I might not feel as chaotic or disorderly. In turn, my grip on the worldly control around me might lessen.

Establish a Routine

When feelings of being out of control get too much, the best thing to do is grab onto the life raft of things we can control. That would be our daily routine. By establishing a routine, we lull ourselves with the fake sense of being in control, as if manipulating a baby to choose one option by making it look better than the others.

Let's face it, humans are creatures of habit. We very rarely change our routine. If I have been washing my dishes in the same pattern (wash, rinse, dry) for the whole of my life, I probably won't change it anytime soon. It's the familiarity of the actions that we crave, especially when living in a world full of unpredictability. When establishing a routine, we may find ourselves feeling a little less out of control as we know what is coming next, we know and expect the series of events that are about to ensue. I can now decide what I choose to do, instead of having to roll with the punches of life as usual.

It has been proven that establishing a healthy routine that includes room for relaxation and preparation for the unpredictable can increase mental health and reduce the anxiety of having to make effortful decisions. It has also been proven to decrease overthinking because of the absence of stress. Routines are the most basic forms of planning; it eliminates the thoughts of panic of *When will I get it all done?* It ensures lack of sleep is a thing of the past and completely eliminates poor time management that leaves room for error without, causing catastrophic consequences in which we may find ourselves back at square one.

Chapter Takeaways

Control is an illusion and cannot be established over every aspect of our lives. There will have to be things in our lives that challenge our character development. However, we have now learned how to deal with feelings of disorder.

- Forget the illusion that I have control over every aspect of my life.

- Stop trying to control every aspect of my life.

- Be mindful of my thoughts, behavior, and feelings.

- Be in tune with my feelings and thoughts; acknowledge them and behave accordingly.

- Establish a routine to minimize the feeling of chaos.

Chapter 4:

Find the Root of the

Problem

When solving problems, dig at the roots instead of just hacking at the leaves. –Anthony J. D'Angelo

Every single impactful thing in our lives leaves a mark on our hearts or souls in remembrance of its passing. Like the scars on our bodies, not all of them are connected to just bad memories. Many of the gashes on our legs carry joyful memories of riding bikes with our friends, or the small cuts on our hands remind us of going fishing with dad. Along with those memories, the worries of our lives will also leave their mark.

But unlike a fingerprint that stays true to its form, our worries will spread like ink over paper and cloud every aspect of our lives until they haunt us even in the haven of sleep. If we allow ourselves to add fuel to the fire, we will find ourselves unable to smother it. Overthinking is the surfer dude that rides in on the wave of self-consciousness and stays to wipe out the shred of self-confidence we have left.

But how do I stop myself from subconsciously opening the door to more overthinking? The best thing to do for myself and everyone else around me suffering from the symptoms of my overthinking, is to pinpoint the root of the problem. *Where does it all stem from? Why is it a trigger?* are questions I ask myself.

Identifying Triggers

Overthinking can't just come into existence without something triggering me. There is always a cause to the jumpstart that gets the cycle going. It could be anxiety about work, underperformance in other aspects of my life, fear of socializing and being cast out, or even rejection. Anxiety and fear are very common triggers of overthinking and can be identified and resolved with simple strategies.

Root Cause Analysis

Root Cause Analysis (RCA) is the fancy way of saying "find the cause of the problem" in order to find effective and appropriate solutions. If I can trace my overthinking "track record" back to the beginning and pinpoint the exact moment that triggered me, I can put avoidance techniques in place to cut down overthinking on that specific subject altogether. This is an effective way to completely eliminate the recurrence of the problem in the future, rather than just curing the "symptoms" of it.

For example, if I find myself anxious about driving and almost cause an accident by accidentally swerving into the lane right in front of another car, I may continue the rest of my drive replaying that image in my head. Progressing from that initial thought, I will start to overthink my driving abilities and how they affect the people around me, if I am a bad driver and why I might be one, and it goes on. Once again, I am venturing into the land where problem-solving is nonexistent.

There are three goals to the RCA that I can use to anchor myself in the moment, before overthinking can commence. The first goal is to pinpoint the exact cause of the problem. I swerved into the wrong lane and almost caused an accident. Second, I need to realize ideas and strategies on how to fix the problem or learn from it. I won't suddenly swerve the car again if I can help it. Third, apply what I learned from the problem to prevent further recurring of the same problem in the future.

The Root Cause Analysis makes use of core principles that guide the effectiveness of its methods. The following core principles being the following:

1. Focus on identifying the root cause and resolving it rather than just "treating" the symptoms.

2. Treat the symptoms for short term relief, but do not let the deeper wound fester.

3. Acknowledge that there might be more than one root cause and apply these methods accordingly.

4. Focus on the *how* and *why* of the situation, rather than who was responsible or involved.

5. Find the appropriate evidence to support claims of the root cause of my overthinking.

6. Gather enough information to make an informed decision and take correctional action.

7. Generate ways how the root cause can be prevented in the future.

When making use of the Root Cause Analysis, it is important to do it with the mindset to solve the problem rather than just identify it. It has to be approached with the intention to take action against the problem that is causing me to overthink.

The Five Whys Strategy

Referencing back to the swerving example, we'll use that to demonstrate the process of the Five Whys Strategy.

First Why: Why did the guy honk at me and flip me the finger? Because I swerved into his lane and almost caused an accident.

Second Why: But why did I swerve? Because there was a piece of rubble in the road that could have damaged my car.

Third Why: Why was there a piece of rubble in the road? Because there was a construction truck in front of me, loaded with materials and a few pieces fell off.

Fourth Why: Why was there a construction truck on the highway? Because he was delivering materials to a construction site.

Fifth Why: Why didn't I do a controlled evasive maneuver? Because it was too sudden.

The Five Whys strategy is like talking to a toddler: They're always too inquisitive.

As we can see, the method does not place the blame on anyone by using aggressive questions such as *who did it?* or whose fault it was. It simply asks the necessary questions I need to pinpoint the exact cause of my overthinking and eliminate it by eliminating the anxiety left over from the scene.

In the future, I may be able to avoid this scenario by changing lanes (safely) when driving behind a construction truck because of the lesson learned on that day. Identification is equivalent to prevention. Case in point. Every time I use these methods, the answers will come quicker and become clearer to the point where I will no longer overthink a scenario and rather find a solution right away.

The Five Whys method is a base to start on. If I find myself to be a more inquisitive person by nature, I can use up to a 100 Whys in my unique situation as long as I use them effectively in order to eliminate the recurring problem.

Change Analysis

In the situation of the aforementioned out-of-control feeling, Change Analysis is the perfect method to identify the roots and prevent them, similar to the RCA. The Change Analysis is based on identifying the root cause of the problem by studying the changes that lead up to it. This method is most effective when there are multiple root causes that are unable to be identified by using the Root Cause Analysis. As we not only study the timeframe based on the specific day the problem occurs, but we also now go back further in time to identify what led up to the cause.

First, I'll record and analyze every potential cause leading up to the event in which the overthinking occurred. The cause likely stemmed from my past; depending on how I contributed to its evolution, it may have grown to become a root cause problem. Afterwards, I'll categorize my influence on the cause and its evolution into a root cause. For example, internal influences, such as anxiety regarding a certain scenario, may have given life to overthinking. Once I have identified the potential events that added fuel to the fire, I must next determine the events that have worsened the root cause (like the anxiety mentioned before). Finally, I'll heal the root cause to avoid overthinking and completely obliterate the chance of it happening again.

Chapter Takeaways

In this chapter, we have explored every single strategy needed to potentially eliminate overthinking completely, pinpointed the exact cause of our overthinking both in the past and current times of our lives, and how to heal the festering wounds that cause recurring overthinking over the same scenarios to keep happening. The strategies include

- identifying what triggers my overthinking.

- making use of the Root Cause Analysis to trace the root cause of my overthinking problem.

- applying the seven core principles of the Root Cause Analysis to properly address the problem.

- making use of the Change Analysis to investigate the historical origins of my cause root problem.

- finding a permanent healing and solution to my root cause, to ensure the prevention of overthinking in the future.

Chapter 5:

Become a Participant, Not an Observer

Do more than belong: participate. Do more than care: help. Do more than believe: practice. Do more than be fair: be kind. Do more than forgive: forget. Do more than dream: work. –William Arthur Ward.

I have lost confidence due to overthinking. I have not only lost confidence in myself, but in what I can do, what I can offer to the people around me, and how important I am to the world around me. Each of us has a part to play in this world, and at one point, I was very certain and confident in mine. I went from being a participant to an observer over the span of a few years and due to an unhealthy cycle of overthinking.

Overthinking, as mentioned before, has a very big impact on our minds. So how do I go from observer to participant in a few steps, not only in my own personal life but in the environments around me? It's not easy or comfortable, but it's doable.

Steps to Improve Your Will to Participate

One day, I'm walking by a gym and see the trainer offering a 50% discount off all sporting goods at *Nike* to any civilian willing to try and review his workout routine and diet. I'm a sports fan, and I just saw a limited edition Lebron James NBA sweater at *Nike* just a few weeks ago. Coincidence? I think not. So, I give it a try. Step one has been completed. I have actively participated in the challenge. There's nothing more to it than that it seems.

But there is. I have to complete the challenge. And now that the heat of the moment has passed and I've had time to think about it, I keep finding excuses not to do it. I won't go because of either lack of confidence in my skills, or I don't have the right clothes. I'm worried I might look stupid when I work out. I'm not as experienced as the other people at the gym, so I might start to feel inadequate. Look familiar? Yes, I am overthinking this. So, let's look into how I can overcome the overthinking of this scenario.

Addressing the problem of the lack of skills. If I am an athlete, I have indulged in the irrational fear that overthinking has placed upon me. Because I am an athlete, I am fit and more than capable of finishing the challenge if done correctly and within my own boundaries. To find security in myself and my skills once again, I need to reroute my brain to remember all of the things I am physically capable of.

1. Do I have the endurance to complete this task? Yes.

2. Have I done something like this before? Yes.

3. Do I have the physical capacity to attempt and maybe succeed at this task? Yes.

4. Do I have a disability or injury that may stop me from completing this task? No.

It takes simple questions to restore confidence in myself. My mind just needs to be reminded of what I have already achieved to make me believe that I can do it again. The true problem is not the actual challenge of participating, but the effort of convincing ourselves of something that we don't believe.

Overcoming Irrational Thoughts

Starting Small

There are stepping stones to this journey. I have to rebuild what overthinking tore down, and it won't be done overnight. Reusing the examples above, we'll start with the diet.

I have to follow the strict regimen the trainer has prescribed in his challenge, without a day of dieting in my history, but that doesn't mean I have to start cutting every single unhealthy thing out of my diet all at once. I can start small by adjusting only one meal a day if his diet is too much to handle all at once. For example, if the trainer advised chicken breasts and egg yolks for dinner, I could start with having just chicken breasts. If he advised me to only eat two times a day, I can start eating less but as frequently as before and slowly work my way toward his goal. For example, having only one sandwich as opposed to two, but snacking on healthy foods throughout the day.

Tips to make the above healthy eating easier is to avoid any cravings at all or minimize the amount of food usually consumed in one sitting. If my way home from work is filled with fast food joints, I'll take another route to avoid the struggle. If my routine is to gulp a gallon of Coca-Cola down before bed, I'll try a glass instead. The same can be applied to the training schedule. If I am unable to complete six sets of fifteen, I'll try to complete eight sets of ten. The same amount of work is being done, but within my own boundaries. It's all about finding ways to eliminate the overthinking that plagues the activities I participate in. By applying the tips above, we have actively eliminated the stress of the diet by making use of evasive techniques to make it easier.

The same can be done with the inadequacy in the gym problem. If I feel unskilled in comparison to the "gym bros" that film themselves and basically live in the gym, I can go to the gym when it's quieter. Less people are likely to see me then. Or I can enlist a training buddy to show me the ropes; that will automatically make it more fun for me and I won't feel as embarrassed. If I'm an introvert, I can search popular videos showing tips and tricks to excel in the gym. Crisis, avoided. Mission, accomplished.

Use Peer Pressure as a Motivator

I am the type of person that sometimes lacks the ability to motivate myself. There is nothing wrong with it, but it does complicate some things in my personal life. Therefore, using peer pressure is the perfect way to get myself going. Because if I can't do it for myself, I can do it to avoid the judgment of my friends.

To a certain degree, an overthinker is always worried about what people might think of them. Whether it be family, friends, or total strangers, they will worry about it in some form or the other. If they are someone that relies heavily upon words of affirmation from a loved one, they will do anything it takes to satisfy the need, as it motivates and drives them to achieve what they need to. It is perfect if they are like me, motivated by the sheer terror of someone being disappointed in me.

In the example used above in terms of inexperience, I can use it as a motivator to keep going to the gym and get better. In the end, I have completed the task, I am now a very skilled gym-bro, and all of the fears I originally had have vanished. I have successfully overcome the overthinking that had initially stopped me from participating.

Chapter Takeaways

In this chapter we discussed how overthinking influences our will to participate in things we normally would, how it influences our confidence and belief in ourselves, and how it impacts our thought patterns. The strategies include

- overcoming irrational thoughts that have been brought forth by overthinking.

- reestablishing confidence in myself.

- taking small steps and making use of evasive strategies to simplify the journey.

- using peer pressure and my fear of judgment as a form of empowerment to get things done.

Chapter 6:

Manage Your Stress

Be a life-long learner. Whether you are seeking to achieve peace and harmony, learn a new technology to do your work faster, or design a strategy to blow your competitors out of the water, retraining is a pivotal way to strengthen your knowledge and realize your goals. –Susan C. Young

It is no secret that stress is one of the main contributing factors to overthinking. It can be described as the artery of overthinking, as every single overthinking thought in our minds can be linked to some form of stress we have. It is also no secret that the internet's ways of "having a bubble bath" or "lighting a scented candle" doesn't help anything. All it does is just move an already stressed and overthinking person from one room to another just with an added vanilla scent and bubbles to add some pizazz.

There are actual techniques, both physical and mental, that can effectively lessen both the effects of stress and lower the levels of stress itself. If we can lower our levels of stress, we can effectively lower the amount of overthinking.

The Four-Point Strategy

Avoid

Avoid the crisis. Take control of the things around me. If I know my car takes longer to start on colder days, I'll get up earlier on snowy days to give myself the time to struggle with my car without being late. Likewise, if I know I don't get up easily in the morning, I'll do all of the preparation for my morning routine (lunch, work supplies, showering) the evening before to leave room for the extra five minutes of sleep I crave.

If there are certain aspects in my life that I know for sure make it more difficult, I need to take preventative measures to ensure I don't cause myself the stress of worrying about the situation beforehand and avoid the difficulty the situation might bring. On the other hand, if there are other things causing me stress, like tasks in the upcoming weeks or days, I might consider labeling them unimportant for the time being, to save myself from the scurrying caused by the chaos of scrambled priorities. It doesn't mean that the tasks will stay unfinished, they are just being prioritized accordingly, to allow myself the room for breathing and relaxation.

The avoidance technique is based on creating preventative measures to avoid the crisis in which stress might occur. In doing so, I have completely eliminated the chance of overthinking happening for a certain situation, and actively solved the problem before it even happened.

Alter

If I cannot completely avoid a crisis that causes stress, the next best thing is to try and alter the course of it. In many situations, I might find myself in a crisis because I didn't take preventative measures to avoid it in the first place as it will sometimes happen in the unpredictable course of life. Even then, it doesn't mean that I *have* to be caught up in the stress of it.

Be willing to compromise. If I set myself up to accept any changes that might occur, I can lessen the effect of the shock and stress that I might undergo should the unexpected happen. I can compromise on the "strictness" of my routine; for example, I might be a little more open to taking another route and getting home later than expected to avoid getting stuck in the traffic that will derail my whole evening. Things are not always supposed to go according to plan because that's how life works. However, we can alter how we react to the unexpected in a way that minimizes the amount of stress we feel in the situation. From that, no overthinking can occur, and things can go as planned (mostly).

Balance my schedule. Working hard is great. It's a great way to achieve my goals faster, improve my skills, secure a sustainable income, and maybe secure myself a promotion in the future. It's also one of the best things to avoid overthinking, as my mind is too busy to worry about anything at the moment besides the work in front of me. But there needs to be a healthy balance between work and play to avoid any burnout. A stress burnout is quite common in recent times due to corporate companies raising the standard of "good work" every year.

We are expected to produce new and unique ideas that have never been done before in a world where a simple Google search can generate any ideas we might dream of, generate new ways of income for the company, generate ways for the company to keep reinventing their image to fit the evolving times of the modern world. We are expected to reach insanely high targets in sales, be available 24/7, make ourselves adapt according to what the company needs, and maintain that standard of work every day.

Sure, the standard is manageable, but it still causes insane stress on us as people. We are not machines designed to exceed in our jobs only. We are human beings who crave being in the sunny outdoors and socializing with others. We have urges that need to be quenched such as a night of partying, going on a vacation, or taking a nap for the first time in a long time. They seem to forget that and definitely won't forgive it. Therefore, it is up to us to do the relaxation on our own while still juggling their demands. We owe it to ourselves to make time in the chaos for a little playtime like reading, painting, jogging, partying, scrapbooking, and every other hobby we can think of. Doing what we enjoy that is separate from the work we do every day (however much we might like it) is the best way to minimize stress centered around our work.

Adapt

Adapt to the crisis as it is happening. Review the situation, take perspective of the direness of the situation, and make a decision based on that. When I am extremely stressed about something and I have no clear reason why, I try to assess where the stress is coming from outside of the situation. It may come from external factors such as a bad day, events recurring out of my control and stress in general, or it is a reaction to the other stressful situations in my life at the moment.

If it is about external factors, I try to look at the picture as a whole. For example, in the situation of a long line at the bank, I'll take the opportunity to catch up on some reading, phone a friend, or organize my emails. Instead of worrying about how long it's taking, I find what else I can do with this time. There are two positives to this thinking. One, my emails will be organized, I will have caught up with my reading and I will have reconnected with a friend; two, I have completely avoided overthinking by evading the stress that this scenario could have caused. In the heat of a crisis that we can't do anything about, it's better to adapt.

Be grateful for the present moment, no matter how dire. In every aspect of our lives, there is always something to be grateful for. In this instance, it may be that we are equipped with the resources to be able to solve most of our problems. In other cases, it's good to just be grateful for the breath in our lungs or the reflection time we get to have in times of waiting (like traffic, for example). Maybe just being grateful for the simple things in life, like having a job to stress about, having friends to call during a mental breakdown, having the ability to even do anything ourselves at all is enough. Gratitude does wonders for a weary heart. It can inflate deflated optimism and put fresh air in the lungs of our mental health.

Accept

Accept what is happening at this moment. We as people, sometimes try too hard to change things to fit the mold we want them to, it's only natural. We try to alter situations that are meant to be just the way they are. We try to make everything fit into the convenience of our routines and schedules. We tend to forget that it's not the end of the world if these things don't go the way we want them to. In the case where I cannot pinpoint the reason or solution for my stress, I give it a good old "It is what it is," and move on. That's the best thing to do in a situation where stress is just stress—no cause, no solution, and no expiry date.

Accepting the moment for what it is will lessen the effects of the stress regarding the situation and over time, cause it to vanish completely. If it does have a cause, but we cannot find the solution after days of self-reflection, it is most likely the situation that will solve itself or teach us a lesson. Every situation is meant to be experienced; the difference is whether we decide if we want to Avoid it, alter it, adapt to it, or accept it, lessening stress altogether.

Chapter Takeaways

Managing our stress is one of the best ways to eliminate the effects of overthinking and avoid over thinking altogether. It is not easily managed, as there are a lot of things to stress about in modern day life, but by using the few strategies discussed, we might make a difference.

- Make use of the Four A's for stress management:

    o Avoid—Avoiding the crisis and in turn avoiding the stress that comes with it.

    o Adapt—Adapt to the crisis to minimize the effects of stress being experienced.

    o Alter—Alter the course of the crisis to avoid the stress it could have caused.

    o Accept—Accept the crisis for what it is.

Chapter 7:

Modify Your Response

Small shifts in your thinking, and small changes in your energy, can lead to massive alterations of your end result. –Kevin Michel

We have all had a moment where we've said some things we shouldn't have, made impulsive decisions in the heat of the moment, or reacted in ways that cannot be fixed. It's human nature to react out of emotion. If we didn't have emotions, we'd be dead inside and have no drive to do anything. There would be no purpose to anything in life or to anything we did. Regardless, there is no changing the fact that we have emotions, but there is changing the way we use them. We can empower them into actions.

It's easy to lose control of our feelings. It's easier to lash out at someone we love and feel sad over things we can't change. It's easier than putting in the work to evaluate our feelings and create healthier ways of "feeling" them. However, that's not what mental and emotional growth requires. It requires conscious action to better the course of our reactions.

Let's say I lashed out in anger at my little brother after having been fired from my job. The anger wasn't directed toward him even if he did ask me to play cars with him one too many times. However, it was about the blatant fact that I had gotten fired and didn't know how to properly respond to the situation and address those emotions.

In situations where we find ourselves unable to respond in a gracious way, there are strategies in place that can be used to alter the route of our responses for the better, and to achieve a clearer perspective.

Take a Breather

I need to ask myself three vital questions before reacting in a certain way that might not add positively to my intent.

1. How is this situation making me feel?

    - To pinpoint what emotions are being experienced at this moment

2. Why do I feel like this?

    - To pinpoint if the cause and the reaction are correlating to the situation in front of me

3. How do I want to respond to this?

    - To pinpoint the appropriate way of processing and reacting to this situation

- To pinpoint how I can go about fixing my emotions if they are not contributing to my response in the right way

If these questions can be answered truthfully and with the right intent, they should be able to rewire our minds from reacting emotionally, to gaining a clearer perspective and making decisions accordingly.

Step Away

Rewiring the mind, as we have seen, is not as easy as it sounds. We are not computers that can be "reset" to act in the right way. One preventative measure to ensure the avoidance of an outburst, is to simply walk away from the situation. I may have to think along the lines of, *I will not utter a word back to a back-talking inferior; I will not spank my very naughty child; I will not act in a manner that is beside the person I am or want to be.*

Stepping away from a scenario will help us clear the steam from our ears, regroup what we are trying to communicate in reaction to something, and spare the loss of progress on overthinking. We all know overthinking will commence if I react in a way that could jeopardize my relationships.

Celebrate the Small Wins of Today

It's no small feat to respond differently than what we are used to. The effort that comes with breaking a lifelong habit, is one that is commonly overlooked. If I am an anger-driven person and respond with kindness and patience today it should be celebrated. If I am a negative person and respond with positivity to a very unpleasant situation, I am celebrating it. Even responding with little phrases like, "It's okay," someone bumping into me, or "Don't worry about it, everyone makes mistakes," to an accident should be celebrated as the biggest win on the planet.

It doesn't matter how I celebrate it, whether it be writing about my progress in a journal, messaging a friend about my progress, or treating myself to something that I feel I deserve as a reward, as long as I acknowledge the significance of my progress in becoming a better person for myself. Anything of the mind that has successfully been altered by ourselves is to be celebrated. It may improve our relationships, and people's perceptions of us, our perception of the happenings around us. It can improve the way we see the world, vanquish overthinking completely, and leave it as a thing of the past. The mind is greatly rewarded with words of affirmation, about it and ourselves. It wants to be nurtured and loved like any of us would want to be, it wants to be accepted and trained. The mind is a beautiful thing, a tool that can be used to build a better 'me', and a weapon against overthinking. The mind is the multitool of the century, it just depends on what we decide to use it for.

Chapter Takeaways

The way we respond to certain situations and people is the first thing that is noticed about us. If we react negatively to every inconvenience, we may be viewed as negative by others and it might affect the relationships in our lives. But if we can control how we react and modify our response to be one we can be proud of, that contributes to the growth of our character and the health of our minds; it can alter our lives as we know it. The strategies used include

- taking a breather and ask myself the 3 important questions.

    1. How is this situation making me feel?

    2. Why do I feel like this?

    3. How do I want to respond to this?

- stepping away from the scenario to gain clarity on the situation and control over my emotions.

- celebrating the small wins and improvements that are slowly making a change in my life.

Chapter 8:

Why Distraction Is Not

Always Helpful

I needed something--the distraction of another life—to alleviate fear. –Bret Easton Ellis

Distraction is not always a bad thing. In fact, in some cases, it is the only thing that works. Distracting our minds from the memories of a bad day or sparing ourselves the cringe of an embarrassing moment can be rewarding. There are many positive aspects to the art of distraction, but when it comes to overthinking, it can actually worsen the problem. In every other situation, distraction is the perfect thing to

- recharge our minds.

- expand our perspectives.

- regroup and assess the problem at hand.

- reward ourselves after a day of hard work.

The problem arises when the reward stops being one and overthinking has become so unavoidable that not even our favorite shows or comical Facebook fails can stop the endless loop in our mind.

The act of distraction, also known as avoidance coping, is perfect for temporary relief. However, we may do more harm to ourselves than good. Avoidance coping makes use of strategies like procrastination and passive-aggressiveness in place of real, problem-solving techniques to avoid having to confront big issues or problems we might be facing in our lives. It may have worked for a while but, as discussed earlier, it is better to confront the deepest root of the problem rather than distract ourselves from it.

Distraction is a form of procrastination from working on improving the problem of overthinking. If we do not take active steps to ensure its total disappearance from our lives, we may always be stuck with an unending cycle of constant worry, anxiety, and overthinking.

Coping Mechanisms

Every person copes with specific situations in their own unique way. It can either be with confidence and problem-solving in their own thought-train or with fear and the use of avoidance techniques that potentially lead to procrastination and the worsening of the problem. There are two main forms of coping.

Approach/Active Coping

Approach/active coping is an active problem-solving effort directed at the problem itself and the issues that may have caused the problem, generally associated with more "adaptive" people. It is structurally used for attempting to reduce stress. It is the most beneficial coping mechanism to the person. It confronts the problem with the intent of erasing it from the "board" completely and minimizes the effects it has on the person in this exact moment. It is also a great learning opportunity to the person who makes use of this strategy as the lessons learned can be applied to similar problems.

Avoidance/Passive Coping

Avoidance/passive coping includes behaviors that attempt to avoid the confrontation of the problem directly and distancing oneself from possible stressors entirely. This coping mechanism is an unhealthy way of dealing with problems and is most often associated with negative personality traits, harmful activities, and poorer results. Sadly, when seeking the temporary bliss of the coping mechanism, people tend to forget that letting it alone can add more stress. Only if nothing can be done about the stressor then is it beneficial to the person making use of its strategies.

Chapter Takeaways

In this chapter, we discussed the unhealthy avoidance techniques that may be used for the help of processing a potential problem. We have learned that there are two different coping mechanisms used to potentially worsen overthinking or eliminate it completely.

- Distraction is of no help to the minds plagued by overthinking.

- Two different types of coping mechanisms include

  ○ approach coping

  ○ avoidance coping

- How each coping mechanism can contribute/eliminate the problem and the recurrence of the problem at hand.

Chapter 9:

Popular Strategies to Overcome Overthinking and Why They Don't Work

To think too much is a disease. –Fyodor Dostoyevsky

In this chapter, we will discuss the most popular strategies that can be used to avoid overthinking. Most of the tips that can be found on the internet are extremely helpful and can almost always stop the cycle of overthinking completely. But just like anything on the internet, there are harmful tips as well. These strategies are good for you to a certain extent, and within moderation. Without the right balance, it will not be beneficial to anyone.

Popular Strategies and Why They Don't Work

Living in the Moment

When overthinking is running its course in our minds, it's hard to "live in the moment". We are so caught up in the cycle, that it is hard to rely on the moment alone to get us out of the fog. It is better to make use of a myriad of things, along with "living in the moment" to solidify the complete drawback from overthinking and returning to the goal of problem-solving.

"Living in the moment" suggests returning from the land of overthinking to the present moment and all of the factors that play into it like where you are, who you're with, and so on. In the present moment, the problem is still at large. Therefore by "living in the moment," we return to the problem as it was before, only this time there are no solutions at the ready and we are back at square one. Making use of correctional strategies like the RCA strategy, before returning to "living in the moment," we can effectively pinpoint the cause of the problem, and from there find a solution to the problem, rather than just returning empty handed.

Asking Yourself the Right Questions

It is one of the strategies mentioned from before, and it can potentially help me to stop overthinking, but only when it is done the right way. If I ask myself the wrong questions, I will not get to the root cause of the problem, pull myself back from overthinking, nor find a solution to the problem. I will only be answering questions to myself for fun, and the problem remains stagnant in my mind.

For example, if I find myself in the scenario of overthinking the project report due tomorrow and feel like it has no "meat," or that it is unprofessional and may not be what the company is looking for. I may then consider either doing it all over or try to silence what may only be the anxiety of overthinking. I'll try the latter, for the sake of my own benefit—as it is almost always the overthinking taking the lead and not me.

Now that I've made the decision to confront the overthinking part of my problem, I'll make use of the questions previously mentioned in Chapter One and Seven. I can either use the problem-solving core questions or I can modify my response to the situation. I can decide. If I modify my response, I might realize that the problem is indeed not as big as I initially thought and review the project one more time before submitting it. Or I can solve the problem as a whole and silence the self-doubt my mind is feeding me.

If I ask myself unnecessary questions, it can potentially worsen the overthinking already in place, and never confront the root of the problem directly. Relating to the example above, I can think of questions such as *Why am I stressed about this report? Because I am afraid it's done incorrectly. Is it the correct report based on corporate guidelines? I am unsure.* Here, we have only established the problem and why it is a problem, but no solution was found, and it will likely continue to be a problem in the future. These strategies are effective, but only when used properly.

Chapter Takeaways

In this chapter we discussed two of the most popular strategies to overcome overthinking and why they might not work for everyone. While they can also tie into some of the strategies we have discussed earlier, if they are not used correctly, they can further complicate the problem.

- I learned why living in the moment is a temporary solution that only leaves me smack bam in the middle of the problem once again.

- I learned why answering the wrong questions does more harm than good and made sure I ask the right questions.

Chapter 10:

The Art of Self-Confidence

The moment you doubt whether you can fly, you cease forever to be able to do it. –J.M. Barrie

Everything in this world is to be done with even the smallest shred of self-confidence. The confidence to walk up to a stranger and ask for their number, to start a conversation, to attempt to chase our dreams, or to do something as simple as eating alone in a restaurant. All of these scenarios make use of the tiniest bit of self-confidence, otherwise we'd all be hole up in our homes with no social interaction. That is the importance of self-confidence; nothing can be done without it.

Every person on the planet earth deserves to have unwavering self-confidence. In situations where we don't, I think it's only fair that we be equipped with the tricks to establish self-confidence right then and there. The lack of self-confidence can burden any person, no matter what status or age, and it can hinder the joy of new experiences. Luckily for us, there is a sea full of tips and tricks to use in order to establish the unwavering confidence we so badly crave.

Establishing Unwavering Self-Confidence

The definition of self-confidence is the attitude we have toward our skills and abilities, the acceptance of our flaws and weaknesses, and the faith in ourselves. It influences the amount of success we have in our lives, and it can impact the way we process any happenings over the span of our lifetimes.

If I am a confident person, I won't react as badly to the harsh reality of truth and criticism. I won't find myself doubting the relationships in my life so often, nor will I lack the ability to establish boundaries regarding those relationships. I won't lack the desire to participate in things and "shoot my shot" in the work environment and everyday life. I will automatically be positive-minded and able to make decisions better, as well as adapt to the things around me easier than before. But if I lack the self-confidence needed to achieve the above mentioned, I can use the strategies below to boost my self-confidence in order to achieve "I'm the best thing since sliced bread" status.

Comparison Is the Root of All Disaster

I have found myself in the position of comparing myself to others too many times. There is always a bigger fish in the sea, a guy with bigger muscles, a girl with a prettier smile, or a co-worker with a better pitch than mine. There is always going to be something we all want for ourselves or want to change about ourselves. Unfortunately, it isn't going to happen.

I am never going to be just like my brilliant co-worker Jason, or bright-smile Britney. I am never going to have muscles as big as Mason, the gym bro, or hair as golden as Kiara's. It is a fact of the world; and why would I want to be like anybody else in the first place?

We are all made to be uniquely ourselves. If everybody were designed to be the same, it would be extremely boring. There would be no competition, no opposition, no funny friends and serious friends, no way to distinguish ourselves from the group. We would all be made up of the same traits, same thoughts, same opinions, same psychological structure, and nobody would dare to be different. We'd all be one person and I personally don't see the fun in that.

The first way to stop myself from shattering my self-confidence is to stop comparing myself to others. If I can manage to stop finding fault in myself, I can give my mind the chance to discover the *remarkable* things about myself that I never recognized before. I can get to know the deepest version of myself, discover the things I love, the things I despise, the things I admire, and how I portray myself to the world. These things are done with the elimination of comparison.

Knowledge Is Power

Humans are simple creatures. In cases where we struggle with confidence, we might surprise ourselves by engaging in situations where we have something to add to the experience. If we have knowledge about a certain subject, we might be more confident to engage in a conversation about it than other kinds of conversations. Because of the simple fact that we *know* we can add value to the conversation, and because of the knowledge we have of this subject, we avoid the risk of making a fool of ourselves. This automatically boosts our confidence in this specific social setting, in turn building up "immunity" to self-consciousness in recurring social settings.

If I don't find myself to be an extremely knowledgeable person, then building a wealth of knowledge can boost my self-confidence, as I will have more ground to stand on should the opportunity present itself. If I am able to engage in the subject where I can add to the conversation, I will be more likely to engage in conversations in the future, with more confidence than before.

Fake It 'Til You Make It

If all else fails, I find myself putting on the mask of false bravado. Forcing myself to look people right in the eye in conversations, making myself speak a bit louder in the face of intimidation, and forcing myself out of my comfort zones is the best way (to me) of gaining the fake confidence I have sold to people.

Sometimes all of the strategies of the internet and self-help books aren't enough, and the last thing one can do for oneself is to fake confidence until it is a true part of oneself. There is nothing wrong with having a lack of self-confidence. Social media has made sure that that is the case for most people. But there *is* something wrong in not doing anything about it. We all deserve the chance to love ourselves so unconditionally that we attract what we believe we deserve. We all deserve to make peace with every aspect of ourselves whether good and horrible. We only have ourselves, and to be so utterly satisfied with who we are is a gift that can only give ourselves.

Failures Aren't Faults

In order for me to reach the height of my self-confidence, I need to realize that failures are meant to happen in order for growth to take place within me. If I never make mistakes, I will never learn, and I can never improve and grow into the person I want to be. Failure in my household makes me a better housemate; failures as a person make me want to grow and be a better person. There is beauty in failure, even though it sucks more than anything. If I am a bad housemate in terms of cleanliness and keep forgetting to do my chores, I'll try to be neater, or remember to wash the toothpaste from the sink, or I'll make sure to wash the dishes before they get on my household's nerves.

Next time, I'll work twice as hard for twice as long to make sure I beat my co-worker in the race for the promotion. Next time, I'll put in more effort to see my friends before they get upset. In the end, I will have grown from it and with the acceptance of my failures as a part of the process of life; I will become more confident as a result.

Preparing for a similar situation that I have failed in before will boost my confidence because I know what to expect and what is expected of me. Therefore, failures are the building blocks of confidence.

Chapter Takeaways

There is power in the art of self-confidence. We are well-adjusted, better at decision making, and we actually understand and accept ourselves when our self-confidence is high. The age of self-consciousness has come to pass. By making use of the strategies above, we can all jump on the bandwagon to a more confident self.

- Self-confidence is the acceptance and knowledge of one's abilities, capabilities, strengths, and weaknesses.

- Higher self-confidence improves character in the sense of taking risks, going for the action, and engaging in social interactions with more ease.

- I should stop comparing myself to others and make room for the extraordinary features inside myself to be acknowledged.

- I need to grow my knowledge in order to build confidence in social settings.

- I can fake it until I make it, and the confidence becomes a reality.

- Remember that failure can be a confidence boost if I allow it to teach me.

Conclusion

Tell me and I forget, teach me and I may remember, involve me and I learn. –Benjamin Franklin

The aim of this book is to equip us with the strategies needed to rewire our minds and our thinking to overcome the symptoms, effects, and cause of overthinking. It has also taught us the tips and tricks we need to get our self-confidence back and keep it. We have learned

- the science behind overthinking and how it affects our brains.

- how to change the narrative in our heads to be beneficial to us by using certain strategies, which include to

  o make use of the five senses.

  o be self-aware.

  o focus on problem-solving.

  o talk to someone.

- how to look toward what's coming and shattering the comfort of the past.

  o freedom of forgiveness

- o importance of balance

- o stop obsessing over mistakes

- how to focus on what we can control and let go of what cannot be controlled.

  - o Mindfulness.   How   mindfulness regarding our thoughts and feelings can in turn control how we choose to react.

- how to find the root of the problem that causes overthinking.

  - o Identifying triggers. Making use of the Root Cause Analysis, the Five Whys Strategy, and the Change Analysis to pinpoint root causes.

- how to become a participant to eliminate the lingering fear caused by overthinking.

- how to manage the stress that triggers the cycle of overthinking and how to minimize stress as a whole.

- how to modify our response to scenarios in order to avoid the trigger that could cause overthinking.

- why distraction is not always the most helpful in the scenario of overthinking.

- popular strategies and why they can be disproved.

- the art of self-confidence, how it adds to the quality of my life and how I can increase self-confidence.

This book is the perfect weapon to enter the battlefield of overthinking with. It discusses the triggers and causes behind overthinking while simultaneously equipping us with the correct strategies to avoid it in the future and equips us with the needed tips to build our self-confidence to a point where we are able to function properly without the hindrance of self-doubt. This book has delved into the science behind our overthinking problems and given our minds the weapons needed to protect ourselves from the claws of unhealthy mentalities. Rome wasn't built in a day, but by applying what we learned in this book, we might start stacking the bricks of the journey to mental health.

Healing has to start from deep within and with a desire to completely eliminate overthinking from becoming problematic again. The responsibility to want to heal the deep inner wound that allows for overthinking lies with us.

We are the wielders of the double-edged sword that is overthinking, and we decide which edge to use.

References

Anonymous. (2022, March 26). Avoidance coping. Wikipedia. https://en.wikipedia.org/wiki/Avoidance_coping

Barrie, J. (2014). QuoteCatalog.com. https://quotecatalog.com/quote/jm-barrie-the-moment-you-b7Kk3A7

Baumeister, R. F., Campbell, J. D., Krueger, J. I., & Vohs, K. D. (2003). Does Self-Esteem Cause Better Performance, Interpersonal Success, Happiness, or Healthier Lifestyles? Sage Publishing. https://journals.sagepub.com/doi/pdf/10.1111/1529-1006.01431

Boyes, A. (2019). How to Stop Obsessing Over Your Mistakes. https://hbr.org/. https://hbr.org/2019/02/how-to-stop-obsessing-over-your-mistakes

Cadman, B. (2018, January 17). Dopamine deficiency: Symptoms, causes, and treatment (S. Falck, Ed.). Www.medicalnewstoday.com.

https://www.medicalnewstoday.com/articles/3
20637

D'Angelo, A. (n.d). Brainy Quote.
https://www.brainyquote.com/quotes/anthony
_j_dangelo_105339

Dostoyevsky, F. (1864). Quoteslyfe.
https://www.quoteslyfe.com/author/Fyodor-
Dostoyevsky-Notes-from-Underground-The-
Double-quotes

Ellis, B. (2005). Quoteslyfe.com.
https://www.quoteslyfe.com/author/Bret-
Easton-Ellis-Lunar-Park-quotes

Ellison, R. (1992) Quotes of Famous People. (Invisible
Man). https://quotepark.com/works/invisible-
man-4125/

Franklin, B. (n.d). Brainy Quotes.
https://www.brainyquote.com/quotes/benjami
n_franklin_383997

Goh, G. (2018). Your Thoughts Matter: Change Your
Thoughts and Change Your Destiny. In Google
Books. Partridge Publishing Singapore.
https://books.google.co.za/books?hl=en&lr=
&id=XWZ6DwAAQBAJ&oi=fnd&pg=PT5&d
q=how+failures+in+life+help+to+shape+your
+destiny&ots=Pnq9d6I6nl&sig=OJpBADBft1I
W-

e7aExfQnUigFJM&redir_esc=y#v=onepage&q
=how%20failures%20in%20life%20help%20to
%20shape%20your%20destiny&f=false

Goldsmith, B. (2010). 100 Ways to Boost Your Self-Confidence: Believe In Yourself and Others Will Too. In Google Books. Red Wheel/Weiser.
https://books.google.co.za/books?hl=en&lr=&id=Ad5EDwAAQBAJ&oi=fnd&pg=PA9&dq=improve+self+confidence+ways&ots=1TOiMaBbVC&sig=dLwLpEkr4UoIno64XmG53md-AeY&redir_esc=y#v=onepage&q=improve%20self%20confidence%20ways&f=false

https://www.facebook.com/WebMD. (2005, April 27). Tips to Reduce Stress and Sleep Better. WebMD;   WebMD. https://www.webmd.com/sleep-disorders/tips-reduce-stress

Koyenikan, I. (2015). Goodreads Quotes. (Goodreads). https://www.goodreads.com/quotes/7139973-the-mind-has-a-powerful-way-of-attracting-things-that

Loehr, J. (2008). The Power of Story: Change Your Story, Change Your Destiny in Business and in Life. In Google Books. Simon and Schuster. https://books.google.co.za/books?hl=en&lr=

&id=XIaloNelSRYC&oi=fnd&pg=PA1&dq=h
ow+failures+in+life+help+to+shape+your+de
stiny&ots=9336G0qyhu&sig=aFCXpKl_UGeF
IjYzdFxOFXw2vQg&redir_esc=y#v=onepage
&q=how%20failures%20in%20life%20help%2
0to%20shape%20your%20destiny&f=false

Lupien, S. (2012). Well Stressed: Manage Stress Before
It Turns Toxic. In Google Books. John Wiley &
Sons.
https://books.google.co.za/books?hl=en&lr=
&id=8alUnwqYSr4C&oi=fnd&pg=PR9&dq=
manage+stress&ots=27qtwQlqI8&sig=A-
6CHTmdNYtvPFNLe4dzAyLKK88&redir_esc
=y#v=onepage&q=manage%20stress&f=false

Mayo Clinic Staff. (2020, August 18). Exercise and
stress: Get moving to manage stress. Mayo
Clinic. https://www.mayoclinic.org/healthy-
lifestyle/stress-management/in-depth/exercise-
and-stress/art-20044469

Michel, K. (2013). Quoteslyfe.com.
https://www.quoteslyfe.com/author/Kevin-
Michel-Moving-Through-Parallel-Worlds-To-
Achieve-Your-Dreams-quotes

Miglani, B. (2013). Embrace the Chaos: How India
Taught Me to Stop Overthinking and Start
Living. In Google Books. Berrett-Koehler
Publishers.

https://books.google.co.za/books?hl=en&lr=
&id=C2ZRKBDSZ_EC&oi=fnd&pg=PP2&dq
=how+to+eliminate+feelings+of+chaos+in+t
he+mind&ots=Vdoneu3_3s&sig=EiIRiSrJvan0
JXb3L6JILuGMB3Q&redir_esc=y#v=onepage
&q=how%20to%20eliminate%20feelings%20of
%20chaos%20in%20the%20mind&f=false

Morin, A. (2019). 5 ways to start boosting your self-
confidence today. Verywell Mind.
https://www.verywellmind.com/how-to-boost-
your-self-confidence-4163098

Patterson, K. (1977). FreebookSummary. (Bridge to
Terabithia, p.32).
https://freebooksummary.com/bridge-to-
terabithia-quotes-with-page-number-118176

Potts, Y. (2019, November 13). The Science Of
Overthinking. The Science of Overthinking.
https://www.woroni.com.au/words/the-
science-of-overthinking/

Saleh, D., Camart, N., Sbeira, F., & Lucia Romo.
(2018). Can We Learn To Manage Stress?
https://journals.plos.org/plosone/.
https://journals.plos.org/plosone/article?id=10
.1371/journal.pone.0200997#ack

Smith, G. (2021). The Book of Overthinking: How to
Stop the Cycle of Worry. In Google Books.
Atlantic Books.

https://books.google.co.za/books?hl=en&lr=
&id=3PrwDwAAQBAJ&oi=fnd&pg=PT8&dq
=side+effects+of+overthinking&ots=7LAIStO
pCC&sig=IYmozojsJgC1qkSz5-
X4rk8a680&redir_esc=y#v=onepage&q=side
%20effects%20of%20overthinking&f=false

Sparks, D. (2019, April 24). Mayo Mindfulness: Try the
4 A's for stress relief.
Https://Newsnetwork.mayoclinic.org/.
https://newsnetwork.mayoclinic.org/discussion
/mayo-mindfulness-try-the-4-as-for-stress-
relief/

Tableau. (2019). Root cause analysis, explained with
examples and methods. Tableau Software.
https://www.tableau.com/learn/articles/root-
cause-analysis

Ward, W. (n.d). Quoteslyfe.com.
https://www.quoteslyfe.com/quote/Do-more-
than-belong-participate-Do-more-4535

Wilding, M. (2021, February 10). How to Stop
Overthinking Everything. Harvard Business
Review. https://hbr.org/2021/02/how-to-
stop-overthinking-everything

Young, S. (2017). Quoteslyfe.com.
https://www.quoteslyfe.com/author/Susan-C-
Young-The-Art-of-Preparation-8-Ways-to-Plan-

with-Purpose-Intention-for-Positive-Impact-quotes

www.ingramcontent.com/pod-product-compliance
Lightning Source LLC
Chambersburg PA
CBHW071212120626
46546CB00006B/2528